HEROES of COVID-19

Written by Nick Barnsby

Illustrated by Anya Bialeska

Children's Futures Publishing Group

I would like to thank Rachael Akinlawon for inspiring
me to write this story and her children and foster children
for their help and advice in acting as my focus group of children
and young people and making me more understanding and more brave.

Dedicated to the memory of

Sidney Roy Edwards 1927-2020

David Alexander Edwards 1962-2020

And all those families affected by the Covid-19 virus.

First edition published 2020 by Children's Futures Publishing Group.

ISBN 978-1-8381231-0-9

Once apon a time in a land far, far away
a new form of life came into being.

Some people did not believe it and some said it was a spell by evil wizards that had jumped out of its bottle by mistake.

Other people said a serpent had slithered into a fish market and created this new life.

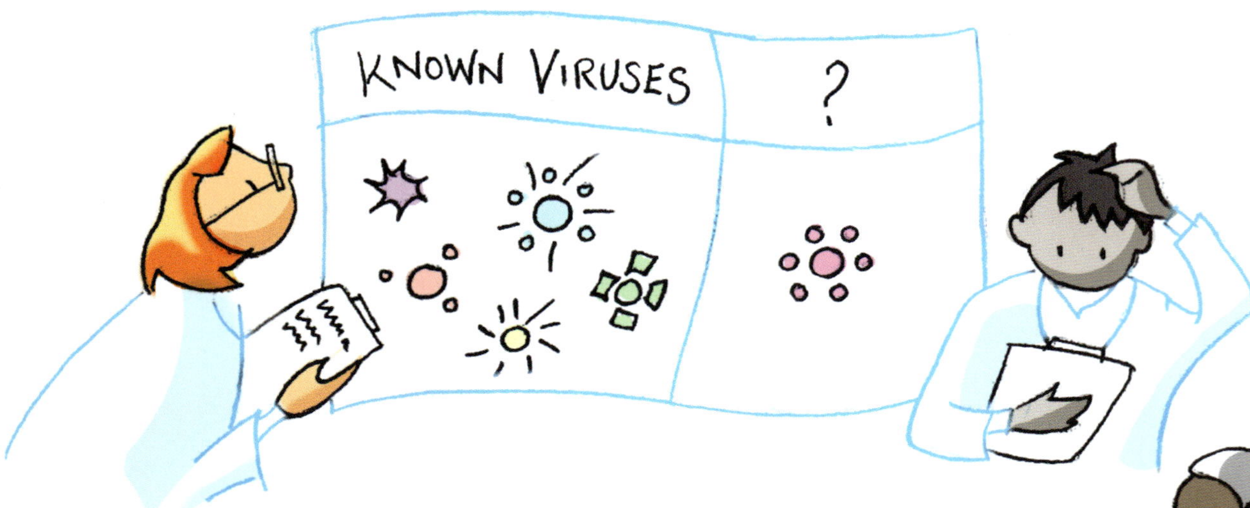

Scientists said it was a mutation of an existing corona virus

Some mutations are good.
Mutant turtles are good mutants and
Spiderman and X-Men are all good mutants.
Drinking milk is something that stone age
man could not do but most of us can do,
because of a good mutation.

But this mutation was bad,
it made people ill,
it was a virus and people could catch it
just like they caught a cold.

The leaders of all nations had a think about what to do.

Some leaders still didn't believe it and thought they would never catch it. Others quietly prepared. Some men who were leaders thought they were too strong and argued over whose fault it was but some wise women leaders got ready early before the virus arrived.

Scientists called it

which was a new word specially made up that belonged to no nation so that nobody would get the blame,

but the leaders of nations still argued about whose fault it was anyway.

It was a cunning virus, lots of people caught it and didn't even notice they had got it.

Most people who got it did not get very ill.

They got on aeroplanes and went on holidays and spread the virus all over the world.

The virus was spread when people coughed or sneezed or sometimes when people who were ill touched others but you couldn't see the virus so people did not know if they had it or were spreading it around.

Animals did not catch the virus.

Thelma and Louise were two chickens that had been on holiday and they did not catch it.

Claudia and Fiona were lambs that were born and played happily in the fields and they did not catch it.

Squee and Abberdasser were cats who ignored it altogether

Bees were too busy and buzzed and made honey.

Henry the peacock continued to show off his tail, and all of his wives laid eggs in appreciation.

But when people caught it, sometimes if they were old, or sick already, some of them got very ill.

Very sadly some people died.

The leaders of the nations decided that
something had to be done.

Scientists looked into their test tubes to see if they could find a cure.

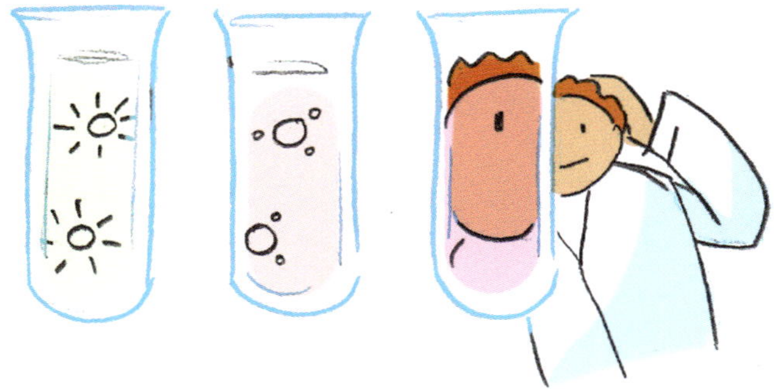

Some scientists tried other medicines out that worked for other things to see if it would cure covid.

Some tried rose hip syrup,
but that didn't work
as it wasn't really medicine at all.

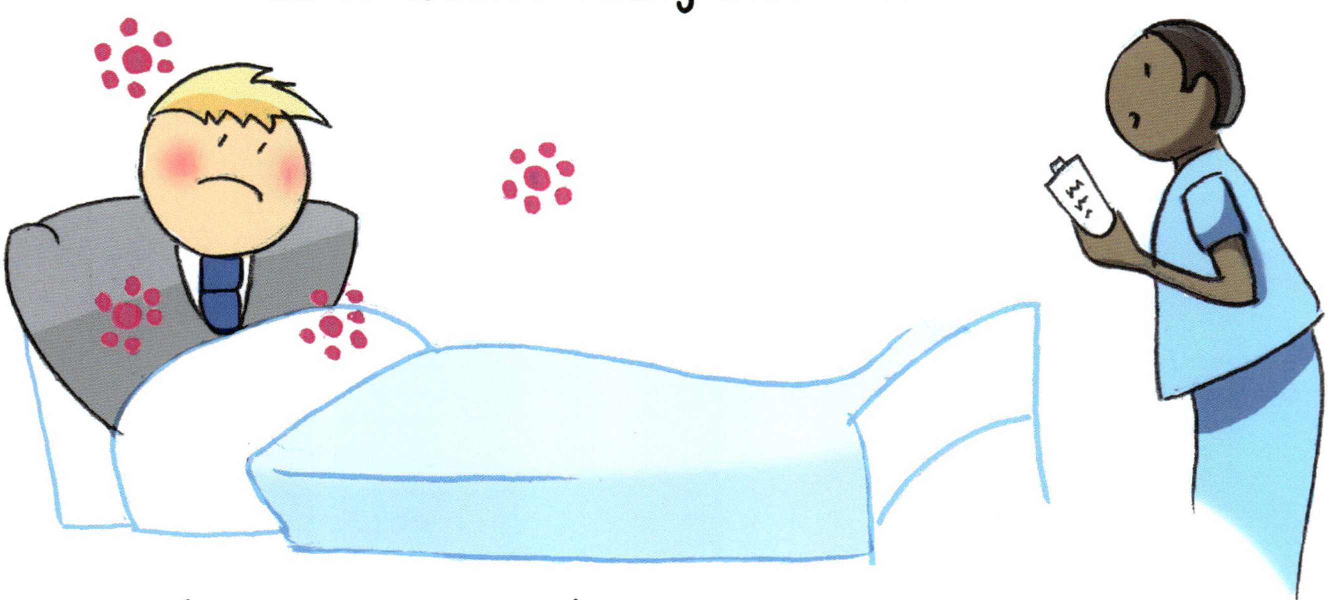

One leader caught the disease himself,
just to illustrate that we were all in this together,
and he had to go to hospital, but nobody could find a cure.

Then they all had the same idea.

"I know" they said "everybody can stay home,

then they will not meet with any other people

and people will not catch the virus and it will go away".

This was the best idea they had.

But some people were already ill in hospital and they couldn't stay home so the leaders of nations said that Doctors and Nurses could be Heroes and continue to go to work to look after them.

And they were allowed to wear masks and wear aprons which were like cloaks worn on your front and they were all like Superheroes.

But doctors needed other people to help them in the hospital so...

ambulance drivers

and cleaners and cooks

and porters who helped wheel patients around and all of the hospital workers became Heroes too.

And hospital workers needed to travel to the hospital and bus drivers and train drivers became Heroes.

And the children of the hospital workers had to go to school while they were at work and teachers became Heroes too.

And even if people stayed at home they still needed to eat

so food shop workers and van drivers and lorry drivers became Heroes too.

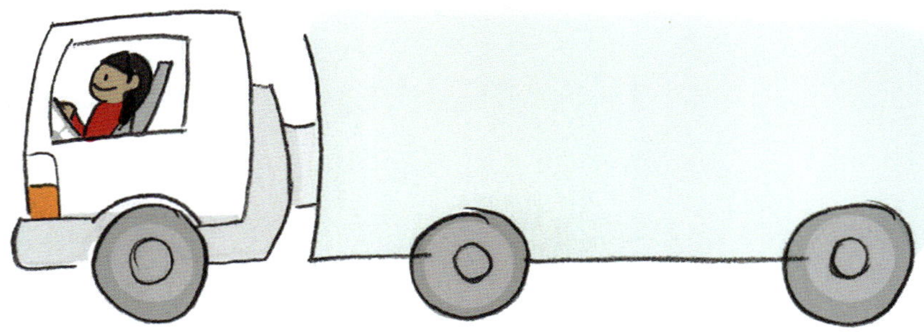

And extra people volunteered to go shopping and check up on people who were old or ill who could not go to the shops and they became Heroes too.

Even Social Workers became Heroes which they were very pleased about because they were Heroes all the time but nobody had ever called them Heroes before.

And some Mummies and Daddies and Foster Carers stayed at home and looked after children and had to teach them at home and they became Heroes too.

Children stayed home and didn't go out to do the things they liked doing and all children became Heroes too.

Most people know someone who is a Hero, even if they did not wear a special costume it still counted that they were a Hero too.

And all the
people in all the lands
stood at their windows
and on their doorsteps and
clapped and made noise and
banged on saucepans

to show how pleased they were to have so many Heroes looking after them.

Children drew rainbows and put them up in their windows

to remind everyone that one day everything

would be better.

One group of Heroes were completely forgotton,

they worked in homes full of old people and locked themselves inside to try and not let the virus in and did not go out at all, so they were nearly completely forgotton about until somebody reminded the leaders of the nations that they were Heroes too.

Some people could not do their usual work but made things to help people get better so people who usually made racing cars and vacuum cleaners made machines for hospitals instead

and others made uniforms for nurses and facemasks to help stop sneezes and coughs from spreading the disease.

Some people stayed at home.

Lots of people already had masks but some masks did not work, Batman had a mask but it did not cover his mouth so wearing a batman mask did not help.

Spiderman had a good mask because it covered his nose and mouth.

Superheroes had the biggest sneezes so they all had to wear masks and some other Heroes had to wear masks too but small children only have little sneezes so they do not need to wear a mask at all.

One man who was already a Hero from the war

became a Hero all over again,

he was very old but

he walked slowly

up and down his garden

one hundred times to celebrate his one hundreth birthday

and people all gave him money so he could give it to the

Doctors and Nurses.

Some men who were good at climbing mountains

ran up and down stairs all day for a whole week

because they did not have their own mountain

and the wives of these men remain Heroes to this day.

As people stayed at home animals came out.

A flock of mountain sheep took over a small town.

People saw more wildlife and noticed the air was cleaner.

People thought about how they could keep the enviroment safe when life went back to normal

So people stayed home and only went out to be Heroes or to exercise and tried to stay away from other people so that they could not catch the virus and the virus would go away.

At the start a lot of people were ill and had the virus but when people stayed at home, less people caught the virus and other people got better

and the virus began to go away.

When less people caught the virus the leaders of nations decided that people could go out more and that they could play golf and tennis and go fishing and everyone except the fish were very pleased.

In some nations that had women in charge this had been happening all along but some of the leaders of nations who were men pretended not to notice and said it was their idea.

Some children had been going to school all of the time

and when people thought it was safe

more children were allowed to go to school.

All the schools had new rules

about where you could go

and who you could play with

and how close you could sit,

just in case the virus came back.

Some mummies and daddies were very pleased because although they had learned a lot when they were teachers too, teaching was very hard work.

And as the virus went away very gradually everything got back to normal. But it was not quite the same normal as it was before so people called it the new normal.

The leaders of nations continued to argue about whose fault it was and to say that it was their idea that saved people...

but really it was the Heroes who had saved people.

Athough lots of them were secret Heroes.

I think you may have ideas

about who some of the Heroes are.

You can use this page to write a list and draw pictures of some of your Heroes.

Don't forget your name and your picture here.

You are a Hero too!

Printed in Poland
by Amazon Fulfillment
Poland Sp. z o.o., Wrocław

61290526R00021